SPIRITUAL INTERVIEW

with Princess

DIANA

HER MESSAGES, 20 YEARS AFTER HER DEATH

RYUHO OKAWA

HS PRESS

Copyright©2017 by Ryuho Okawa

Original title: "Diana Moto Kotaishihi no Spiritual Message"

All rights reserved

HS Press is an imprint of IRH Press Co., Ltd.

Tokyo

Library of Congress Cataloging-in-Publication Data

ISBN 13: 978-1-943869-23-7

ISBN 10: 1-943869-23-5

Printed in the United States of America

Contents

Preface

The truth of the death of Princess Diana is still in the darkness.

However, the two decades from her death gives us a chance to reveal new reality.

Her death—was it real tragedy or not—shall be understood through reading this book.

Truly, Truly, she is a person of "Love."

And, she still is a seeker of "Real Love."

May Princess of Wales be able to find "Real Love of God"!

I, and we, Happy Science did our best to save her soul.

I hope she will be reborn as a real Goddess through our spiritual conversation.

Aug. 16, 2017
Master Ryuho Okawa

Spiritual Interview with Princess Diana

Her Messages, 20 Years
After Her Death

Recorded Aug 10, 2017
Special Lecture Hall, Happy Science,
Japan

Diana, Princess of Wales (1961 ~ 1997)

A member of the British royal family. Her noble title was Princess of Wales. Third daughter to Earl Spencer. She first met Charles, Prince of Wales when she was working as a teacher's assistant at a kindergarten in London. The two married in 1981. She gave birth to her first son Prince William and younger son Prince Henry. However, due to Prince Charles' extramarital affairs, they lived separately and eventually divorced in 1996. She then put all of her energy into charities toward AIDS patients and removing landmines. She was put in the public spotlight when she began dating several Muslim men such as a doctor and a businessman. During her visit to Paris, France in 1997, she was involved in a car accident while avoiding the paparazzi. Diana lost her life at the young age of 36. Millions of people mourned her death during her national funeral.

Interviewers from Happy Science*:

Masayuki Isono
Executive Director,
Chief of Overseas Missionary Work Promotion Office,
Deputy Chief Secretary, First Secretarial Division,
Religious Affairs Headquarters

Sayaka Okawa
Vice Chairperson,
Chief of CEO's Office,
Religious Affairs Headquarters

Suzuna Yagi
Second Secretarial Division,
Overseas Missionary Work Promotion Office,
Religious Affairs Headquarters

*The opinions of the spirit do not necessarily
reflect those of Happy Science Group.*

1

Late Princess Diana
Asks for an Interview

RYUHO OKAWA

Good afternoon, everyone. I'm planning to invite or summon the spirit of Princess of Wales, as you may know, the famous Princess Diana.

She passed away in 1997, on the 31st of August. So, this month will be 20 years since her death. Everyone in the world has plenty of concern regarding the memories about her and some are still thinking about the secret of her death. Was she murdered or just killed in a car accident? What is her condition now, after she left from this world? What happened to her and what did she see? What kind of atmosphere appears around her? Where does she belong, I mean, in the spiritual world? What kind of dimension[*] is she living in now? Maybe she still doesn't understand what's happened to her. We have a lot of questions about her.

---

[*]According to Happy Science, the Spirit World is divided into dimensions from four to nine in accordance to the levels of enlightenment. The lower part of the fourth dimension is Hell, and the dimensions above the fifth are Heaven. Those with good hearts reside in the fifth dimension, leaders and experts in the sixth, angels in the seventh, great angels in the eighth, and saviors in the ninth dimension. Refer to *The Laws of the Sun* (New York: IRH Press, 2013) and *The Nine Dimensions* (New York: IRH Press, 2012).

To tell the truth, this morning, she already came to see me and asked me, "Is it OK to have an interview with you?" I don't have enough knowledge and I can't come up with a good idea on how to explain and express her emotions or concepts, but you have a lot of knowledge about her, so we just want to challenge and enjoy this spiritual experience with her. I've not yet investigated how she is living now, so this is a riddle, but please make it clear through your questions.

Is it OK to start? OK, then, I want to summon the spirit of Princess of Wales, famous Princess Diana.

> The spirit of Princess Diana,
> Would you come down here
> And answer our questions?
> Princess Diana, Princess Diana,
> Would you come down here?

[*About 15 seconds of silence.*]

2

Why Does She Feel "Lonely"?

PRINCESS DIANA
Hello, hello.

MASAYUKI ISONO
Good afternoon.

DIANA
Good afternoon.

ISONO
Are you Princess Diana?

DIANA
Uh huh, yes.

ISONO
Thank you very much for coming to Happy Science.

DIANA
Oh, Happy Science?

ISONO
Yes.

DIANA
I don't have enough knowledge about your group. Is it OK?

ISONO
Yes.

DIANA
Thank you. Thank you.

ISONO
It's an honor for us to have an interview and ask you several questions.

DIANA
Oh, OK. Please be kind to me.

ISONO
Yes. We are kind.

DIANA
Ah, really?

ISONO

As Master Okawa explained, you came to see Master this morning. My first question is, why did you come to see Master? Do you have anything you wish to say to people?

DIANA

I was invited by your International Division.

ISONO

I see.

[*Interviewers laugh.*]

DIANA

They asked Master Okawa, "Please summon the spirit of Princess Diana," so I contacted.

ISONO

Spiritually? I see.

DIANA

Spiritually, yeah. He is like Tokyo Tower, so then, I could contact him. Yeah.

But it is my first experience. I have some experiences regarding spiritual phenomena, but this is my first experience, so be kind and be elegant about your questions.

ISONO
Certainly.

DIANA
So, [*while clapping a few times*] please, please, please.

ISONO
Thank you. Twenty years have gone since you passed away, and the people all over the world remember you, love you and admire you.

DIANA
Thank you.

ISONO
The news media aired a special report about you recently. Since 20 years have passed by, how do you feel now?

DIANA
A little lonely.

ISONO
Lonely?

DIANA

Lonely and a little sad. I feel some kind of sadness. But abandonment is essential. I was told like that, so... Hmm. This is a chance to improve my spiritual condition. Are you a famous priest or something like that?

ISONO

Not so famous. But we are priests.

DIANA

Please give me God's Love.

ISONO

Could you explain more specifically about your feelings? You said you have sadness and loneliness. Why do you feel so?

DIANA

I belong to the English Church. It's one kind of Christianity. I was Princess of Wales, and now, I still am. But after I divorced, I made, as you know, some kind of boyfriends. Islamic people. One to four, or more [*laughs*].

My situation is a little difficult to explain. Should I go to the Heaven of Christianity of England? Or, should I go to the Heaven of Islamic people? My heart is almost broken. I have some attachments to my kids, of course. Who am I? What am I? Religion is very important. You are Happy Science?

ISONO
Yes.

DIANA
What is Happy Science? Oh, it's very difficult. Are you Buddhism? Christianity? Islam? Or, I don't know, the Red Cross-like group?

ISONO
Happy Science is a universal religion.

DIANA
Universal religion?

ISONO
It goes beyond all differences of religions. In short, we connect Christianity and Islam. We are a kind of bridge that connects those religions.

DIANA
Is it possible? I mean, is it OK for the Princess of Wales to appear through Happy Science?

ISONO

It's not a problem. No problem at all.

DIANA

Really?

ISONO

Yes.

DIANA

It's OK?

ISONO

Absolutely.

DIANA

You are not Islamic people, I know, but are you Shintoism, Taoism, or something like that?

ISONO

Actually, our God is called El Cantare[*].

DIANA

Oh, too difficult.

---

[*] The highest spirit and the Supreme God of the terrestrial spirit group who has been guiding humanity since the beginning of Earth. A part of His core consciousness is living on earth as Master Ryuho Okawa. Refer to *The Laws of the Sun* (New York: IRH Press, 2013).

ISONO

Is it too difficult?

DIANA

Too difficult for me. Do you have permission through God or the Church of England?

ISONO

We don't have any permission from the Church of England, but Master Okawa is a great religious leader.

DIANA

Then, is this officially a good thing? I mean, is this a phenomenon welcomed by the people of the world?

ISONO

Yes, definitely.

DIANA

Really? OK, OK.

3

Who is the Real God?

SAYAKA OKAWA

Thank you for this great opportunity, Princess Diana. We are Happy Science.

DIANA

Oh, you! You are a princess, too.

SAYAKA OKAWA

Thank you so much. Master Ryuho Okawa is trying to unite every religion, so you're very lucky to speak in Happy Science.

I'd like to ask you about the Church of England. As you know, the Queen of England is the top of the Church of England. Do you think the Church of England receives spiritual guidance from Heaven?

DIANA

Oh.

SAYAKA OKAWA

What do you think about...

DIANA
Difficult question! Umm…

SAYAKA OKAWA
Do you have any guidance from the English Church?

DIANA
Umm, it's a great question.

ISONO
Yes, it's a tough but important question.

DIANA
People of England loved me and love me greatly, but in the spiritual meaning, whether God or higher spiritual beings of England like me or not, I'm not sure. So, it is my great concern.

Am I a good person or a bad person? Who judges this problem? I'm not sure. Am I right or not? Am I a good person in front of God or not? But I want to ask, "Who is the real God?" Christian God, English God or Allah? I'm not sure.

ISONO
Hmm.

DIANA

Who decides good or evil? Please teach me.

ISONO

While you were alive, what kind of God did you believe in?

DIANA

Hmm. I'm not sure.

ISONO

You're not sure?

DIANA

I'm not sure.

SUZUNA YAGI

When you were alive, you said in your famous quote, "I'm aware that people I have loved and have died and are in the spirit world look after me." That is a famous quote of yours. So, I think when you were alive, you must have believed in some God. What do you think?

DIANA

Hmm. I am poor at studying, especially theology and philosophy or philosophic regions. So, it's very difficult for me, but I believe in the reality of love and just that

God is love and love is God. In this context, I belong to God, I hope so.

But the definition is very difficult, so please teach me. Am I right or not? Please teach me. Teach me.

4

She Has No Position in the World

SAYAKA OKAWA
After your death, maybe you had some experience in another world. Could you please describe the world you live in now?

DIANA
I live in now?

SAYAKA OKAWA
Yeah.

DIANA
Hmm. I live in now... Hmm, I have no position...

ISONO
No position.

DIANA

…in the world…

ISONO

Where do you think you are now? What kind of world?

DIANA

I have a grave of course, in England, but I am not living in that grave. I mean, the people who died, they are lying under the ground, but I'm not there, of course. But what am I… how should I conduct… or who should I follow…? I'm not certain about that.

So, help and teach me the reality of the spiritual world and this world. Why am I sitting here? Why can I stay here? Why can I answer you? Why can you understand my voice? It's very difficult.

You said 20 years have passed since my death, but I cannot understand what my entity is. Who am I? What am I? How should I live? Am I just dreaming, or am I just lying like a dead person? Please guide me.

SAYAKA OKAWA

Do you see someone else?

DIANA

Hmm?

YAGI

Do you see some people?

DIANA

Some people? Some people... Some people...

YAGI

Or anything you can see around you?

DIANA

[*8 seconds of silence.*] Here? Japan?

ISONO

Yes, here is Japan.

DIANA

Japan? Not England?

ISONO

No, not England.

DIANA

Hmm. Japan. Why can I stay in Japan? I came to Japan three times. But this time, I experienced no flight, and no one escorted me. So, why am I here?

SAYAKA OKAWA
Master Ryuho Okawa can invite spirits.

DIANA
Oh, really?

SAYAKA OKAWA
You are a spirit.

DIANA
Ah, yeah, I know, I know. I know that kind of supernatural people. I know, I know, I know, psychic. I know, I know, I know, I know, I know, I know, I know, I know. I'm dreaming and Mr. Okawa looked though another world and transferred my dream to you? I cannot understand the situation correctly.

SAYAKA OKAWA
Maybe you still exist in England?

DIANA
Really? England? Really?

SAYAKA OKAWA
I don't know. But maybe you are worried about your family. Prince William, Prince Henry or Princess Catherine.

DIANA

I nearly understand that I might be dead, but I can't correctly understand how I can live, still now. I might be some kind of ghost?

SAYAKA OKAWA

Yes.

DIANA

Oh, no! Heavens no! No, no, no, no, no, no, no, no, no, no, no, no, no, no, no. I don't like ghosts. Oh, no, no, no, no, no, no, no, no. It's a dream, dream, dream, bad dream, bad dream.

SAYAKA OKAWA

But you are still thinking.

DIANA

Yeah, yeah, yeah. Hmm. This is Japan.

ISONO

Yes.

DIANA

You are Japanese.

ISONO
Yes. We are Japanese.

DIANA
Oh, why, why, why, why, why, why, why, why? Please answer because because because…

ISONO
Can you understand that you are a spirit?

DIANA
Hmm…

ISONO
Because you don't have your body?

DIANA
Hmm… Partly yes, partly no.

ISONO
Partly no?

5

On the Secret of Her Death and Thoughts on Her Family

YAGI

But at least you understand you are not surrounded by paparazzi, right?

DIANA

Paparazzi! [**YAGI** *Laughs.*] Oh, paparazzi, oh, paparazzi, oh, bad people.

ISONO

Yes, we think that they are very bad.

DIANA

Oh! But I don't have any hatred toward them. I'm still living and...

SAYAKA OKAWA

You actually died in a car accident in Paris, 20 years ago.

DIANA

Car accident? Oh...

SAYAKA OKAWA

Yes. Do you remember the situation? If you remember, could you tell us about the accident?

DIANA

Car accident. There was a car accident and I was carried into the hospital. After that, I'm sleeping, sleeping, sleeping, sleeping, but still living.

ISONO

Yes.

SAYAKA OKAWA

Some people say that you were killed by someone.

DIANA

Killed by... Hmm...

SAYAKA OKAWA

Do you think that is true?

DIANA

I'm not sure, but I felt some kind of evil intention. Hmm...

ISONO

Could you tell who had the evil intention toward you?

DIANA
Maybe secret service or…

ISONO
Maybe MI6[*] or something?

DIANA
Yeah, like that. I was scared about their shadow. Someone was aiming to deprive me of my life after I got a divorce. It's from Charles or…

ISONO
Prince Charles?

DIANA
Prince Charles or…

SAYAKA OKAWA
It's very terrible.

DIANA
He can send some messenger of death…

ISONO
To you?

---

[*] A popular name for one of the intelligence agencies of Britain, the Secret Intelligence Service. It is assumed that they take on espionage missions overseas. The 007 movie series has James Bond playing the role of an MI6 secret agent.

DIANA

Yeah.

SAYAKA OKAWA

Is it true that it was because your "friends" were Muslims?

DIANA

It's not so dangerous. But my princes belong to the royal family of England. I am the mother of my princes. It would be a problem if I converted to Islam, so it's a very dangerous thing to the English church system. It's enough reason for them to murder me. I am not sure, but Prince Charles could make such kind of plan. Of course, the real person who was disguised as paparazzi is MI... ?

ISONO

Six?

DIANA

Six? MI6 or not, our 007 or not, I am not sure. But I was always chased by someone.

SAYAKA OKAWA

Both Prince William and Prince Henry were deeply sad that they lost you, so do you have any message for them? Do you have any advice for them and Princess Catherine?

DIANA
[*Sighs.*] Oh. Prince Charles, you said?

ISONO
No, no, to your children.

SAYAKA OKAWA
Prince William and Prince Henry, your children.

DIANA
Henry?

SAYAKA OKAWA
And your child's wife.

DIANA
Catherine? Catherine is very kind to me. I feel like that.

ISONO
She respects you very much.

DIANA
Yeah, yeah. My former husband [*clicks tongue*]…

SAYAKA OKAWA
Can you forgive him?

DIANA
No.

SAYAKA OKAWA & YAGI
No?

DIANA
No, definitely no. No, no, no.

ISONO
So, do you still hate him?

DIANA
I don't hate him, but I believe that he's a devil.

YAGI
Oh…

ISONO
He's a devil?

DIANA
Ah, I think so.

6

The English Church and The Royal Family Had Some Bad Experiences in History

SAYAKA OKAWA

I learned about the history of England. The starting point of the Church of England was Henry VIII, "the bad king." So, maybe the English royal family had some bad experiences in history?

DIANA

Whether the English Church is formal, I mean, whether it was set up by God or not, I have some doubt about that. Is it a good religion? It's too complicated. I cannot understand through my brain, but is it a true religion, or true faith to God or to Jesus Christ? I'm not sure.

Oh, you asked if I met someone else. I met old kings or old queens in the history of England, but almost all of them were ghost-like people, so I was frightened.

YAGI

You've met them? So...

DIANA
I met some people.

ISONO
So, you met kings and queens in history?

DIANA
Kings, queens.

SAYAKA OKAWA
For example, Queen Anne?

DIANA
Oh.

SAYAKA OKAWA
No?

ISONO
How about Queen Elizabeth I?

DIANA
Queen Elizabeth I? I don't know everyone. Queen Elizabeth I…

ISONO
Or Queen Victoria?

DIANA
Victoria… I'm not sure.

SAYAKA OKAWA
So, do you think some of the kings and queens are still ghosts?

DIANA
Many.

SAYAKA OKAWA & ISONO
Many?

DIANA
Many are still ghosts.

SAYAKA OKAWA
Also, you think your Prince Charles is a bad person?

YAGI
Evil?

DIANA
He is not planning to be a ghost. He is planning to go to Hell.

SAYAKA OKAWA & ISONO
Hell?

DIANA
And become a devil.

YAGI
How about your children?

DIANA
Ah, that's a problem, that's a problem [*sighs*]. I want to save them [*sighs*]. How can I save them? Save the... princes...

7

Unable to Forgive Prince Charles Even Now

ISONO
This might be a difficult question for you, but I'd like to ask, what do you think was your mission? Because you chose to be born into this world. You chose the U.K. and you were born as a noble lady. You got

engaged and married to Charles, Prince of Wales.

DIANA

But I am not qualified to become the Queen of England. I have some questions about this religion. Is England good or not? I don't think every English person is bad, but the starting point of the English Church was an evil one, I think. It's regarding the marriage problem. In my case, also, there were marriage problems.

So, this kind of Christianity is a little different. I want to believe in the true love of Jesus Christ. It's OK. But I can't believe in old kings or queens as gods or priest-like beings. I'm skeptical of them. Royal families are cursed from the starting point. An evil will has started this system. It's a marriage problem, I think. You said Anne?

SAYAKA OKAWA

Yes.

DIANA

Queen Anne?

SAYAKA OKAWA

Yes, who was killed by her husband, King Henry VIII.

DIANA

Almost the same situation! If I had been born at the same time, several hundred years ago, I would've had to be killed by the king or someone else [*sighs*].

They are battling with Jesus Christ, I think. This is the real situation of England's religion. They need some help from the real spiritual world, God or angels. I've not seen any angels. So, the royal family shall end with the Queen now. Charles will be the end of the royal family.

YAGI

So, are you the only one who tried to give love to others in the royal family?

DIANA

Yeah, and I gave my love to the people of the world. As you know, I helped the people who were in poverty, had AIDS or those who lost their hands or legs by landmines. I did such kind of charities all around the world. I did some kind of good things to this world.

I cannot understand the reality of God, but I guess God appears where love is. So, I just want to do something good to the world and I want to give my love to the people in weaker situations. I think that is the duty of the royal family.

But they think a little different. They are thinking

of getting some kind of rights to the subjects, I mean the…

ISONO
People?

DIANA
…people of England. They are seeking pride, money, or prestige, or asking for respect from the world. But my situation is quite different. I think great people should give love, especially to the people who are lacking the way to live happily.

So, I think my deeds were not so bad, but my former husband couldn't understand my thinking and looked down upon me. I had weak points in my brain and in my heart, and was a different person in the royal family, he thought like that. He got remarried to another lover. She was a person who was with him before I appeared. That's not fair, that's rude, that's not the royal road, I think.

He should do some reflection for the sake of God's forgiveness. I think so. But he thinks nothing about that. He thinks his deeds are good deeds or God's deeds. As you said, I am dead. My husband thinks my accident was a punishment from God, like that. So, it's very sad for me. I cannot forgive him even now.

8

Who'll Teach Me
The Truth and Real Love?

SAYAKA OKAWA

Our Master said that love surpasses hatred, so if you cannot forgive him, please forget him.

DIANA

Forget him?

SAYAKA OKAWA

Forget him and think about the people of the world.

DIANA

Oh, but my children.

SAYAKA OKAWA

Ah, children. They look to be good or they look like kind people, so maybe it's not a problem.

DIANA

No problem? Hmm. The reality is that the English Church cannot save me.

SAYAKA OKAWA & ISONO
No.

DIANA
Islam cannot save me. But you can save me?

SAYAKA OKAWA
El Cantare is the same existence as the one who Jesus Christ called "my Father." So, Jesus Christ's Father is El Cantare. If you believe in El Cantare, you can be happy.

DIANA
Hmm… I have no knowledge about that.

ISONO
You believe in the God of love, correct?

DIANA
Yeah, God is love and I feel the Love of God.

ISONO
The name of the God of love is El Cantare.

DIANA
Ah, really?

ISONO
Yes.

DIANA
Ah…

YAGI
Where do you think your love comes from?

DIANA
By nature, by nature. I'm a being who has a lot of love within me and love is like flowers, so I want to give one flower and another flower to everyone who is seeking something from me. That is the duty of the royal family, I think. So, my faith is just a small one, just to believe in the Truth and the real love. I lost the real love and I couldn't find the Truth, so who'll teach me the Truth and real love?

SAYAKA OKAWA
I think you are loved by God.

DIANA
No, I'm loved by the people of the world. I appreciate that and I'm thankful to that.

But I don't really understand or feel God's Love. If God has love and gave me love, I, I, I could, I could... I could have survived my tragedy. You said a car accident and I was killed? Oh, no. Where is God? Where is God's Love? Where is God's Truth? What does it mean?

ISONO
I think that God gives you everlasting life.

DIANA
Everlasting love?

ISONO
Ah, no. Everlasting life.

DIANA
Life?

ISONO
Yes.

DIANA
Oh...

ISONO
You lost your body, but you still have your life. I mean, you can think, you can feel, and you can tell your feelings to the people.

DIANA

Oh…

ISONO

You are still alive. This is one of God's Love, I think.

DIANA

Hmm… Hmm… I still have attachment to my children, and I cannot help thinking about bad things regarding my husband and I cannot think about good things regarding paparazzi.

I want to light up the world and want to be a light of England. In my days, I was a light of the world. People of the world respected me a lot. But the result was a tragedy. I cannot solve this riddle, still now. What were my destiny and my life plan?

SAYAKA OKAWA

You are still loved by people all over the world, and Master Ryuho Okawa said you came from the world of goddesses[*]. So, maybe, you were a goddess.

DIANA

Goddess?

[*] Refer to *Hanei no Ho* (literally, The Laws of Prosperity)(Tokyo: IRH Press, 1999).

SAYAKA OKAWA

Before you were born into...

DIANA

I feel that you are a goddess.

SAYAKA OKAWA

Thank you [*laughs*].

DIANA

I feel, I feel, I feel. I feel or it sounds like that. Some voices from Heaven say that you are a goddess, but I don't know what kind of goddess you are. Religion is very difficult.

9

England Needs Purity, Reflection, And a New Revolution

SAYAKA OKAWA

I am a Japanese soul, so [*laughs*] maybe it's different from your spiritual world, but you have some mission for England or the English people.

DIANA

Hmm… My life is just like Queen Anne of tragedy. It's a history of England, the royal family.

SAYAKA OKAWA

What do you think about Queen Elizabeth?

DIANA

Which one?

SAYAKA OKAWA

The mother of Prince Charles.

DIANA

Ah, Elizabeth. Hmm… Maybe a great mother. But she is the last one, the last light of England.

ISONO

Don't you hope that your child, Prince William, becomes the king of the U.K.?

DIANA

I'm afraid that England will experience another revolution. So, I cannot imagine that the royal family will continue forever. My tragedy, it's a turning point, I think so. There's no truth. There's no love. There's no loyalty. There's no obligation to subjects, so I feel a little different. That's the reason I prefer Islam. They are very religious people whom I love. They seriously believe in God, but we do not.

Our God is the God that was made by a king. It's an authority that the king needs. Our God is just a halo of king system, so there's no mind or heart or something like that. Purity, I mean. So, in England, we need some kind of Puritan Revolution in the near future.

ISONO

Recently, the Islamic people entered the U.K. and there are many Islamic terrorist attacks in the U.K. and the EU, too. What do you foresee in the future of the U.K. and the EU?

DIANA

I don't know exactly about terrorism, but Islamic God

and English God… Ah, it's beyond my imagination, so I'm not in charge of that matter.

But the people of England need purity and pure mind to God and loyalty to God. Islamic people have faith, but they need some kind of realistic and… they must behave themselves. I mean, they are very rude. If they are rude, we, the people who are native to England, cannot respect their religion or their God, so they must be civilized people.

I loved such kind of Islamic person, for example, the cardiac doctor or movie producer. They are great people, and I can have respect for them. But among all of the immigrants of Islamic people, some are undereducated and commit terrorism or things like that. So, it's a very difficult problem. Their God can be misunderstood and we think that it must be the deeds of devils again.

So, we must look through the fruits to see what is true or what is false. We must define through its fruits. I think so.

YAGI
You said the English people have to have a pure mind to God. What do you think they need to do to have that state of mind?

DIANA

They must reflect on these 500 years. It means intrusion and imperialism of Great Britain. They killed a lot of people of the world and they colonized a lot of countries of Africa and Asia, like India. The people of Great Britain were great, but they also did a lot of bad things. So, they must reflect upon that. Is this really the Glory of God, or is this just self-motivation for their own happiness or profits? This is the beginning of the loss of purity in religion. I think so.

Jesus just taught us, "Believe in God, be kind to poor people and love each other." He taught like that. But Great Britain did quite the contrary to that. It's 180 degrees contrary to the teachings of Jesus Christ. So, I cannot believe in Jesus Christ through English, Anglo-Saxon-like church. They are bad, I think. It's just indicated by the behavior of the king, queen or prince. They're selfish, so it's not good.

England is declining in these 100 years. It must be the Will of God. I think so. We need reflection about history; about our bad deeds and about our crimes. I did. I did, for example, get rid of landmines or help AIDS people. These are the deeds of Jesus Christ. The English church and military system made great mistakes in these several centuries, so we are declining in these 100 years. We will continue this decline for another 100 years and at that time, the royal family will disappear from this world like the Japanese royal family. I guess so.

10

Diana's Warning On the Future of The Japanese Imperial Family

ISONO
You mentioned about the Japanese royal family, the imperial family. How do you see today's imperial family of Japan?

DIANA
If they live according to the teachings of God, it will be OK to be accepted by the people. But if their existence is representative of their aristocracy, it will be destroyed by a new political system, I mean a "people first" political system. It's contradictory to that kind of aristocracy, so they will decline and disappear from this world.

SAYAKA OKAWA

So, you think the royal family needs both strong faith to God and kindness to people? Is that right?

DIANA

Yeah. But in the long run, our existence is not essential to our people. They can live happily without the royal family.

So, if we can continue the royal family, we, the royal family, must be the representatives of God. It's the least condition, I mean, the minimum condition to live with people. I don't know exactly how the Japanese royal family is, but for England, the end is coming. I think so.

ISONO

We, Japanese people, are also afraid that the Japanese imperial family will end soon because the starting point of the imperial family of Japan is Goddess Amaterasu*, which means the Goddess of the Sun. We, the Japanese, believe in the Goddess of the Sun. Japanese people want to light up the world as the sun does. We believe that the imperial family or Japanese emperors in history were the descendants of the real God of the Sun.

---

* The Sun Goddess who is the principal goddess of Japanese Shinto.

But in my opinion, the current Japanese emperor doesn't seem to accept this spiritual fact. He wants to abdicate*, and he wants his son, the Crown Prince, to become the next emperor. We are very sad about that.

DIANA

Maybe they also lack the experience of spirituality, or how do I say… some kind of revelation from God. The royal family needs some kind of revelation from God, or needs to understand or accept the revelation from God. It's a condition.

But they want to be secular beings, I mean ordinary people. They want to live like ordinary people and just seek freedom. They think they are prisoner-like existence. It is the starting point of the collapse of a dynasty.

But I heard that the Japanese emperor system is a little different. They're closer than we are, I mean closer to God. If they hate to behave or to be servants of God, that is the starting point of the end of the imperial system. I think so.

We, in England, cannot be the good example for the people. That is the collapse of our myth. I was

---

* On July 13, 2016, Japanese media outlets reported that His Imperial Majesty Akihito showed his intention to the Imperial Household Agency that he wished to abdicate the title, while alive, to the crown prince. On August 8, the emperor's video message was broadcasted on television. The cabinet of Prime Minister Shinzo Abe approved special legislation that would allow the emperor to abdicate just this once.

loved by the people of the world, but it's just like the movie stars or supermodel-like popularity. Not a divine one. So, it's a problem.

SAYAKA OKAWA

Also, in Japan, we have Princess Masako[*].

DIANA

Princess Masako. Oh, I know. I know.

SAYAKA OKAWA

She's a little similar to you. Maybe she has some problem in the imperial family, so can you give her some advice?

DIANA

I want to ask her, "Do you believe in the god of Japan?" That is the starting point.

She went abroad and studied the Western philosophy or thinking, so she must think that the

---

[*] Member of Japanese Imperial Family. Crown Princess. Born in 1963. After graduating from Harvard University, she studied at the University of Tokyo. During her attendance at the University of Tokyo, she passed the entrance examination and entered the Ministry of Foreign Affairs of Japan in 1987. She married His Imperial Highness Crown Prince Naruhito in 1993. Based on her experience as a diplomat, there were high expectations of her attending to royal duties regarding international relations. However, she had difficulty adjusting to life in the Imperial family, which led to her diagnosis of an emotional disorder in 2004 and absence in public affairs. As of August 2017, she continues to receive treatment for her illness.

Japanese emperor system is too old-fashioned and wants to restore or remake the tradition. But it will destroy the long history of Japanese emperor system. Then, keep a clean heart and purity in mind. Believe in God and act as God desires. Behave and be a good example for the people of the country. These are the small conditions to exist in this world as a royal family. I don't know so deeply about Princess Masako, but the main point is not intelligence. The main point is the depth of faith in God. I think so. She must abandon something, and after that, she will receive something from God.

Worldly things are not good for royal people, so she should not think too much of herself and behave like a wise person or a clever working lady. It's not the origin of respectable people. Just have a pure mind, love for the people, and faith in God. Those are the necessary conditions for her to be a good queen.

11

Searching for Her God and Her Religion

SAYAKA OKAWA

Thank you very much. I think you have strong faith in God, so maybe you can go up to Heaven.

DIANA

I'm searching for my God, the real God who teaches me the Truth, who teaches me the real love, who teaches me purity, and who teaches me the difference between good and evil. I'm seeking such kind of religion.

I'm the Princess of Wales, but I'm not more than that. I just got the worldly respect, but I don't have enough connection to the real God. In these 20 years, you said, I have been searching for the real God, the real religion, and the answer to "What is the real religion?" Are Islamic people good or do they have good religion or faith? Or, are Christian people good? Why have Christian people been fighting each other in these several hundred years? I cannot understand.

Your Japanese emperor system, either. Emperor Showa said he was an appearance of God, but after the ruin of the Japanese Great Empire, he said, "I'm a man[*]." But it's not enough, I don't think it's enough. Why did God destroy the empire and kill a lot of people; the Japanese people, Chinese people, Korean people, Russian people, Asian people, and American people? Why did the American god destroy the Japanese empire? You should know the reality about that. So, it's a mystery even for me. Why can the Japanese emperor system continue today?

SAYAKA OKAWA

We also have a problem, of course, so we are now thinking about the Japanese system. Today, you came here and here is Happy Science, so you can learn Happy Science teachings. In the teachings, you can find the Truth.

DIANA

In the U.K., Happy Science is not so famous.

SAYAKA OKAWA

No, sorry. I'm sorry.

DIANA

So, please act more diligently, I mean ardently, and

---

[*] Emperor Showa issued an imperial rescript in January 1946, following Japan's surrender in WWII. In it, he made a statement that is commonly interpreted as his denial of being a living god. The Japanese mass media at the time called this statement, "Humanity Declaration."

teach people about the real religion, the real God and teachings of God. Our people sometimes have a lot of pride and look down upon Asian people, so they cannot receive the correct teachings of the Asian god.

But I also think that racism is bad. It's a bad thing. People are equal. God is equal to all nations. He should be so. The Truth, true love, purity to God, loyalty to God, what is God, who is God, or how is God— if your religion can explain these things correctly, we, the people of the U.K., can understand that.

Our government is always seeking the victory in election and the economic growth only. So, it's not enough. I think so. We need the Truth. We must live up to the Truth. We must approach God. I think so. That is the raison d'être of the royal family. We must be a bridge to God. I think so.

SAYAKA OKAWA

You didn't like racism. That's why all people love you. Thank you so much about that.

DIANA

Be kind to weaker people. The great countries of the world like the United States, the U.K., China, and Russia have a lot of nuclear weapons and they can kill a lot of people of the future. But before that, they should reflect upon their history.

Please think about the equality of worth in people's living. Asia, Africa, Europe, North America, South America, Australia, and other countries. They are equal. Created equal. God loves equally. So, great countries have responsibilities to help weaker people or weaker countries. Never use the strong power to make a slavery system again in the near future. I think so.

12

The Conditions of Real Beauty
By Princess Diana

ISONO
OK. May I ask a little bit about beauty?

DIANA
Beauty?

ISONO
Because you are such a beautiful woman.

YAGI
Yeah, and you are one of the beauty icons and fashion

leaders as well. So, people find you really attractive. We would like to know how to become such an attractive lady.

DIANA

Thanks so much, but I wonder about that. Hmm…

YAGI

Because even though you passed away in such a bad way, people held a national funeral for you. So, you're really loved by people. We would like to know how to become attractive or be loved.

DIANA

Hmm, I'm wondering about the origin of beauty. If it comes from the beauty of the mind, the beauty of the heart, it's correct. But if it is just to attract the minds of men, it is not the real beauty. It is just an illusion or just something to mislead people into the way to Hell. Like my former husband. Firstly, he loved me, but after marriage, he didn't have true love because it meant my beauty was just his accessory. So, he just wanted to show me as a beautiful lady and wanted to be proud of the fact that a prince can get the world beauty. But it's not the real way, I think. We need to be shining inside.

Beauty has two edges. One is to kill people or ruin

people. The other one makes people happier, makes people seek the truth, or gives people good motivation to improve themselves to make this world a utopia or Heaven-like world.

Beauty has two directions, so just look at the origin of beauty. It's very important. If you have some kind of bad intention to create beauty, it will just make an illusion and it will make people fall into a hole, so be careful when you seek beauty.

If your mind is beautiful, you can be beautiful and you can get real inspiration from Heaven. How to act, how to behave, how to choose your clothes, or how to take care of your facial condition or body condition. It can get God's approval. But if you have a bad intention within you, to be beautiful is to disguise God's Will, so it will bring another ruin to humankind. I think so.

13

What is the Key to the Goddess' World?

ISONO

OK, the time is almost up, so this is my last question.

DIANA

OK.

ISONO

People of the world still respect and love you, and they call you "People's Queen" or "The Queen of People's Hearts." People are still searching for a message from you, so could you give a message to the people of the U.K. and the people of the world?

DIANA

I guess your group has a new goddess, so your group should show what a goddess is, what the light of Heaven is, and what the light of the world is. People want to see such kind of a new goddess style. I was just a fashion leader and I just had the popularity. Now, 20 years have passed, but I'm still in this condition, just searching for the real God, the real religion, the real beauty, the real love and the real Truth.

Through this conversation, I just felt something sacred from Heaven. I can see the figures of angels and they say, "Your road will be prepared from now on." They say like that.

So, this chance was very good for me. I was not a good princess, but in the near future, I will train my mind and become one of the original goddesses. I want to reach out to the English people and the people of the world.

People will be disappointed at my spiritual interview, but this is just the transit from this world to another world. I am just staying in that kind of station. In the near future, I want to be a guiding spirit of the world.

So, please keep in your mind that Diana's figure in this world is not all of the figure of Diana. Diana, in reality, is the light itself. This is my recognition today. You taught me like that. Just today, I got the key to Heaven, the key to the goddess' world. I am very thankful for your invitation today.

I was wandering around, attached to this earthly world. I want to teach the people of England, "You must seek new religion or spiritual reality. This is your chance. Please, please, please, please make up your mind to learn the new reality of religion. You must restore your traditional religious system. I guess so." To say more than that is beyond my sight, so I cannot say anymore, but I made up my mind, so if I could,

I would be a real goddess.

SAYAKA OKAWA

We will try to spread your message to the world, so don't worry. You're OK.

DIANA

It's OK? Some will be disappointed at my words, but some will find new hope from my spiritual sayings. This is the reality. I will not disguise anymore. This is my reality. I'm just staying at the station to go from this world to another world. This is my position. I'm not a goddess as it is, but in the near future, I will be a goddess and will shed the light to all the people of the world. So, please wait a little more.

I correctly, surely, got some key to Heaven today. Thank you, thank you very much.

ISONO

Thank you very much, too.

SAYAKA OKAWA & YAGI

Thank you very much.

DIANA

To all of you. Thank you.

14

After the Spiritual Interview — Spreading the Right Spiritual View to the U.K. and Around the EU

RYUHO OKAWA

[*Claps once.*] [*Laughs.*] Hmm. How was that?

ISONO

I think her message was very powerful and hopeful for the people of the world. As Sayaka-san said, we will do our best to spread this message to the world.

RYUHO OKAWA

We are not known in England, so this is our chance to spread our Truth to the U.K. and around the EU. It's a very difficult task, but we must do our best. I think so. Thank you very much.

ISONO

Thank you very much, Master Okawa.

SAYAKA OKAWA & YAGI

Thank you very much.

About the Author

RYUHO OKAWA is Global Visionary, a renowned spiritual leader, and an international best-selling author with a simple goal: to help people find true happiness and create a better world.

His deep compassion and sense of responsibility for the happiness of each individual has prompted him to publish over 2,200 titles of religious, spiritual, and self-development teachings, covering a broad range of topics including how our thoughts influence reality, the nature of love, and the path to enlightenment. He also writes on the topics of management and economy, as well as the relationship between religion and politics in the global context.

To date, Master Okawa's books have sold over 100 million copies worldwide and been translated into 28 languages. In addition to publishing books, he continues to give lectures around the world.

Furthermore, Master Okawa is giving increasing impact on a worldwide level, both through live broadcast and TV programs. From August to September of 2016, FOX5 TV aired eight episodes of his lectures in New York, New Jersey, Connecticut and Pennsylvania, inviting many positive feedback.

For more about Master Okawa, visit ryuho-okawa.com

Lecture Broadcasted in Over 3,500
Places Around the World

Since he established Happy Science in 1986, Master Ryuho Okawa has given more than 2,600 lectures. This photo is from the special lecture which was held at Tokyo Dome in Japan, on August 2, 2017. In the lecture titled, "The Choice of Humankind," Master revealed the historical secrets of the creation of humankind, and asserted that humans are now at a crossroads, which is to either choose peace and stability or not. While its natural for countries to defend themselves, he directed that there is another standard on whether the countries defended themselves based on the Will of God. Toward the end of the lecture, Master Okawa declared that above all religions exists the God of the Earth, and addressed to the whole world the importance of humans to stop war and terrorism and harmonize. About 50,000 people attended the main stadium and the event was also broadcasted live in over 3,500 places around the world.

Over 2,200 Books Published

Master Ryuho Okawa's books have been translated into 28 languages and the readership is growing around the world. In 2010, he received a Guinness World Record for publishing 52 books in a year and in 2013, he published 106 books within a year. As of March 2017, the number of books published reached 2,200.

Among them there are also a lot of spiritual messages from the spirits of historical greats and the guardian spirits of important figures living in the current world.

What is a Spiritual Message?

We are all spiritual beings living on this earth. The following is the mechanism behind Master Ryuho Okawa's spiritual messages.

1 You are a spirit

People are born into this world to gain wisdom through various experiences and return to the other world when their lives end. We are all spirits and repeat this cycle in order to refine our souls.

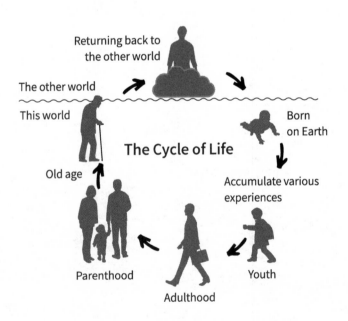

Returning back to the other world

The other world

This world

Born on Earth

The Cycle of Life

Old age

Accumulate various experiences

Parenthood

Youth

Adulthood

2 You have a guardian spirit

Guardian spirits are those who protect the people who are living on this earth. Each of us has a guardian spirit that watches over us and guides us from the other world. They were us in our past life, and are identical in how we think.

3 How spiritual messages work

Master Ryuho Okawa, through his enlightenment, is capable of summoning any spirit from anywhere in the world, including the spirit world.

Master Okawa's way of receiving spiritual messages is fundamentally different from that of other psychic mediums who undergo trances and are thereby completely taken over by the spirits they are channeling. Master Okawa's attainment of a high level of enlightenment enables him to retain full control of his consciousness and body throughout the duration of the spiritual message. To allow the spirits to express their own thoughts and personalities freely, however, Master Okawa usually softens the dominancy of his consciousness. This way, he is able to keep his own philosophies out of the way and ensure that the spiritual messages are pure expressions of the spirits he is channeling.

Since guardian spirits think at the same subconscious level as the person living on earth, Master Okawa can summon the spirit and find out what the person on earth is actually thinking. If the person has already returned to the other world, the spirit can give messages to the people living on earth through Master Okawa.

Since 2009, more than 700 sessions of spiritual messages have been openly recorded by Master Okawa, and the majority of these have been published. Spiritual messages from the guardian spirits of people living today such as Donald Trump, Japanese Prime Minister Shinzo Abe and Chinese President Xi Jinping, as well as spiritual messages sent from the spirit world by Jesus Christ, Muhammad, Thomas Edison, Mother Teresa, Steve Jobs and Nelson Mandela are just a tiny pack of spiritual messages that were published so far.

Domestically, in Japan, these spiritual messages are being read by a wide range of politicians and mass media, and the high-level contents of these books are delivering an impact even more on politics, news and public opinion. In recent years, there have been spiritual messages recorded in English, and English translations are being done on the spiritual messages given in Japanese. These have been published overseas, one after another, and have started to shake the world.

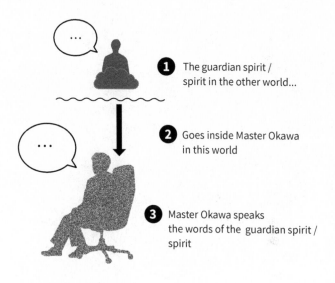

1 The guardian spirit / spirit in the other world...

2 Goes inside Master Okawa in this world

3 Master Okawa speaks the words of the guardian spirit / spirit

For more about spiritual messages and a complete list of books in the Spiritual Interview Series, visit okawabooks.com

About Happy Science

In 1986, Master Ryuho Okawa founded Happy Science, a spiritual movement dedicated to bringing greater happiness to humankind by overcoming barriers of race, religion, and culture and by working toward the ideal of a world united in peace and harmony. Supported by followers who live in accordance with Master Okawa's words of enlightened wisdom, Happy Science has grown rapidly since its beginnings in Japan and now extends throughout the world. Today, it has twelve million members around the globe, with faith centers in New York, Los Angeles, San Francisco, Tokyo, London, Sydney, Sao Paulo, and Hong Kong, among many other major cities. Master Okawa speaks at Happy Science centers and travels around the world giving public lectures. Happy Science provides a variety of programs and services to support local communities. These programs include preschools, after-school educational programs for youths, and services for senior citizens and the disabled. Members also participate in social and charitable activities, which in the past have included providing relief aid to earthquake victims in China, New Zealand, and Turkey, and to flood victims in Thailand as well as building schools in Sri Lanka.

Programs and Events

Happy Science faith centers offer regular events, programs, and seminars. Join our meditation sessions, video lectures, study groups, seminars, and book events. Our programs will help you:

- Know the purpose and meaning of life
- Know the true meaning of love and create better relationships
- Learn how to meditate to achieve serenity of mind
- Learn how to overcome life's challenges

...and much more.

International Seminars

Each year, friends from all over the world join our international seminars, held at our faith centers in Japan. Different programs are offered each year and cover a wide variety of topics, including improving relationships, practicing the Eightfold Path to enlightenment, and loving yourself, to name just a few.

Happy Science Monthly

Happy Science regularly publishes various magazines for readers around the world. The Happy Science Monthly, which now spans over 200 issues, contains Master Okawa's latest lectures, words of wisdom, stories of remarkable life-changing experiences, world news, and much more to guide members and their friends to a happier life. This is available in many other languages, including Portuguese, Spanish, French, German, Chinese, and Korean.

Happy Science Basics, on the other hand, is a 'theme-based' booklet made in an easy-to-read style for those new to Happy Science, which is also ideal to give to friends and family.

You can pick up the latest issues from Happy Science, subscribe to have them delivered (see our contacts page) or view them online.*

* Online editions of the *Happy Science Monthly* and *Happy Science Basics* can be viewed at:
info.happy-science.org/category/magazines/

For more information, visit www.happy-science.org

Contact Information

Happy Science is a worldwide organization with faith centers around the globe. For a comprehensive list of centers, visit the worldwide directory at http://www.happy-science.org or www.happyscience-na.org. The following are some of the many Happy Science locations:

United States and Canada

New York
79 Franklin Street, New York,
NY 10013, U.S.A.
TEL 1-212-343-7972
FAX 1-212-343-7973
Email: ny@happy-science.org
Website: www.happyscience-ny.org

Los Angeles
1590 E. Del Mar Blvd.,
Pasadena, CA 91106, U.S.A.
Phone: 1-626-395-7775
Fax: 1-626-395-7776
Email: la@happy-science.org
Website: www.happyscience-la.org

Orange County
10231 Slater Ave #204
Fountain Valley, CA 92708
U.S.A.
Phone: 1-714-745-1140
Email: oc@happy-science.org

San Francisco
525 Clinton Street,
Redwood City, CA 94062, U.S.A.
Phone/Fax: 1-650-363-2777
Email: sf@happy-science.org
Website: www.happyscience-sf.org

Atlanta
1874 Piedmont Ave. , NE
Suite 360-C Atlanta, GA 30324,
U.S.A.
Phone/Fax: 1-404-892-7770
Email: atlanta@happy-science.org
Website: www.atlanta.happyscience-na.org

Florida
5208 8th Street,
Zephyrhills, FL 33542 U.S.A.
Phone:1-715-0000
Fax: 1-813-715-0010
Email: florida@happy-science.org
Website: www.happyscience-fl.org

New Jersey

725 River Road, #102B
Edgewater, NJ 07020 U.S.A.
Phone: 1-201-313-0127
Fax: 1-201-313-0120
Email: nj@happy-science.org
Website: www.happyscience-nj.org

Hawaii (Oahu)

1221 Kapiolani Blvd., Suite 920
Honolulu, HI 96814, U.S.A.
Phone: 1-808-591-9772
Fax: 1-808-591-9776
Email: hi@happy-science.org
Website: www.happyscience-hi.org

Hawaii (Kauai)

4504 Kukui Street
Dragon Building Suite 21
Kapaa, HI 96746 U.S.A.
Phone: 1-808-822-7007
Fax: 1-808-822-6007
Email: kauai-hi@happy-science.org
Website: www.happyscience-kauai.org

San Diego

7841 Balboa Avenue, Suite #202,
San Diego, CA 92111 U.S.A.
Phone: 1-626-395-7775
Email: sandiego@happy-science.org

Toronto

845 The Queensway Etobicoke,
ON M8Z 1N6 Canada
Phone: 1-416-901-3747
Email: toronto@happy-science.org
Website: www.happy-science.ca

Vancouver

#212-2609 East 49th Avenue,
Vancouver, BC, V5S 1J9, Canada
Phone: 1-604-437-7735
Fax: 1-604-437-7764
Email: vancouver@happy-science.org
Website: www.happy-science.ca

International

Tokyo

1-6-7 Togoshi, Shinagawa,
Tokyo, 142-0041 Japan
Phone: 81-3-6384-5770
Fax: 81-3-6384-5776
Email: tokyo@happy-science.org
Website: www.happy-science.org

Sydney

516 Pacific Highway, Lane Cove
North, NSW 2066, Australia
Phone: 61-2-9411-2877
Fax: 61-2-9411-2822
Email: sydney@happy-science.org
Website: www.happyscience.org.au

London

3 Margaret Street,
London, W1W 8RE, United Kingdom
Phone: 44-20-7323-9255
Fax: 44-20-7323-9344
Email: eu@happy-science.org
Website: www.happyscience-uk.org

Seoul

74, Sadang-ro27-gil,
Dongjak-gu, Seoul, South Korea
Phone: 82-2-3478-8777
Fax: 82-2-3478-9777
Email: korea@happy-science.org
Website: www.happyscience-korea.org

Taipei

No.89, Lane 155,
Dunhua N. Road.,
Songshan District,
Taipei City 105, Taiwan
Phone: 886-2-2719-9377
Fax: 886-2-2719-5570
Email: taiwan@happy-science.org
Website: www.happyscience-tw.org

Brazil Headquarters

R. Domingos de Morais 1154,
Vila Mariana, Sao Paulo, SP-CEP
04009-002, Brazil
Phone: 55-11-5088-3800
Fax: 55-11-5088-3806
Email: sp@happy-science.org
Website: www.happyscience-br.org

Jundiai

Rua Congo, 447,
Jd.Bonfiglioli, Jundiai, CEP
13207-340, Brazil
Phone: 55-11-4587-5952
Email:jundiai@happy-science.org

Nepal

Kathmandu Metropolitan City,
Ring Road, Sitapaila,
Kimdol, Ward No.15,
Harati Marg,Kathmandu, Nepal
Phone: 977-1-4272931
Email: nepal@happy-science.org

Happiness Realization Party

The Happiness Realization Party (HRP) was founded in May 2009 by Master Ryuho Okawa as part of the Happy Science Group to offer concrete and proactive solutions to the current issues such as military threats from North Korea and China and the long-term economic recession. HRP aims to implement drastic reforms of the Japanese government, thereby bringing peace and prosperity to Japan. To accomplish this, HRP proposes two key policies:

1) Strengthening the national security and the Japan-US alliance which plays a vital role in the stability of Asia.

2) Improving the Japanese economy by implementing drastic tax cuts, taking monetary easing measures and creating new major industries.

HRP advocates that Japan should offer a model of a religious nation that allows diverse values and beliefs to coexist, and that contributes to global peace.

For more information, visit en.hr-party.jp

Happy Science University

★ This is an unaccredited institution of higher education.

The Founding Spirit and the Goal of Education

Based on the founding philosophy of the university, "Pursuit of happiness and the creation of a new civilization," education, research and studies will be provided to help students acquire deep understanding grounded in religious belief and advanced expertise with the objectives of producing "great talents of virtue" who can contribute in a broad-ranging way to serve Japan and the international society.

Faculties

Faculty of Human Happiness

Students in this faculty will pursue liberal arts from various perspectives with a multidisciplinary approach, explore and envision an ideal state of human beings and society.

Faculty of Successful Management

This faculty aims to realize successful management that helps organizations to create value and wealth for society and to contribute to the happiness and the development of management and employees as well as society as a whole.

Faculty of Future Creation

Students in this faculty study subjects such as political science, journalism, performing arts and artistic expression, and explore and present new political and cultural models based on truth, goodness and beauty.

Faculty of Future Industry

This faculty aims to nurture engineers who can resolve various issues facing modern civilization from a technological standpoint and contribute to the creation of new industries of the future.

HAPPY SCIENCE ACADEMY
JUNIOR AND SENIOR HIGH SCHOOL

Happy Science Academy Junior and Senior High School is a boarding school founded with the goal of educating the future leaders of the world who can have a big vision, persevere, and take on new challenges. Currently, there are two campuses in Japan; the Nasu Main Campus in Tochigi Prefecture, founded in 2010, and the Kansai Campus in Shiga Prefecture, founded in 2013.

Other Activities

Happy Science does other various activities
to provide support for those in need.

Success NO.1
Buddha's Truth Afterschool Academy

Happy Science has over 180 classrooms throughout Japan and in several cities around the world that focuses on afterschool education for children. The education focuses on faith and morals in addition to supporting children's school studies.

Angel Plan V

For children under the age of kindergarten, Happy Science holds classes for nurturing healthy, positive, and creative boys and girls.

The Golden Age Scholarship

This scholarship is granted to students who can contribute greatly and bring a hopeful future to the world.

Never Mind School for Truancy

At 'Never Mind,' we support students who find it very challenging to attend schools. We also nurture their self-help spirit and power to rebound against obstacles in life based on Master Okawa's teachings and faith.

"You Are an Angel!" project

Happy Science has a volunteer network that encourages and supports children with disabilities as well as their parents and guardians.

The Helen Society

Happy Science supports visually and hearing impaired people to study the Truth. By learning the Truth, they are able to study about this world and the spirit world, make themselves better, overcome their obstacles, and be able to live a bright life.

Future Stars Training Department

The Future Stars Training Department was founded within the Happy Science Media Division with the goal of nurturing talented individuals to become successful in the performing arts and entertainment industry.

New Star Production Co., Ltd. & ARI Production Inc.

We have companies to nurture actors and actresses, artists, and vocalists. They are also involved in film production.

Art and Culture Festival

The Art and Culture Festival is held once a year with the hope of promoting religious art. Winners are given opportunities to further promote their art and pursue their passion.

About IRH Press

IRH Press Co., Ltd, based in Tokyo, was founded in 1987 as a publishing division of Happy Science. IRH Press publishes religious and spiritual books, journals, magazines and also operates broadcast and film production enterprises. For more information, visit OkawaBooks.com.

Follow us on:
Facebook: Okawa Books
Twitter: Okawa Books
Goodreads: Ryuho Okawa
Instagram: OkawaBooks
Pinterest: Okawa Books

Other Books by Ryuho Okawa

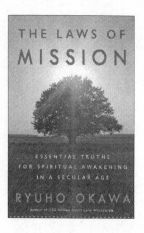

THE LAWS OF MISSION
ESSENTIAL TRUTHS FOR SPIRITUAL AWAKENING IN A SECULAR AGE

In this day and age of advanced scientific and information technology, we are often deluded by a false sense that we know everything. But in fact, many people cannot even answer simple but fundamental questions about life, such as "what's the purpose of our life" and "what happens after death."

In this book, Ryuho Okawa offers integral spiritual truths that bring about spiritual awakening within each of us. This book helps us find the purpose and meaning of our life and make the right decisions so that we can walk on the path to happiness.

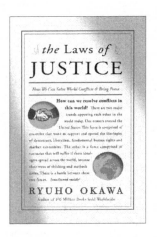

THE LAWS OF JUSTICE
HOW WE CAN SOLVE
WORLD CONFLICTS & BRING PEACE

How can we solve conflicts in this world? Why is it that we continue to live in a world of turmoil, when we all wish to live in a world of peace and harmony?

In recent years, we've faced issues that jeopardize international peace and security, including the rise of ISIS, Syrian civil war and refugee crisis, break-off of diplomatic relations between Saudi Arabia and Iran, Russia's annexation of Crimea, China's military expansion, and North Korea's nuclear development.

This book shows what global justice is from a comprehensive perspective of the Supreme God. Becoming aware of this view will let us embrace differences in beliefs, recognize other people's divine nature, and love and forgive one another. It will also become the key to solving the issues we face, whether they're religious, political, societal, economic, or academic, and help the world become a better and safer world for all of us living today.

THE TRUMP SECRET

SEEING THROUGH THE PAST, PRESENT, AND FUTURE OF THE NEW AMERICAN PRESIDENT

Donald Trump's victory in the 2016 presidential election surprised almost all major vote forecasters who predicted Hillary Clinton's victory. But 10 months earlier, in January 2016, Ryuho Okawa, Global Visionary, a renowned spiritual leader, and international best-selling author, had already foreseen Trump's victory. This book contains a series of lectures and interviews that unveil the secrets to Trump's victory and makes predictions of what will happen under his presidency. This book predicts the coming of a new America that will go through a great transformation from the "red and blue states" to the United States.

CONTENTS

MARGARET THATCHER'S MIRACULOUS MESSAGE

AN INTERVIEW WITH THE IRON LADY 19 HOURS AFTER HER DEATH

On April 9, 2013, just nineteen hours after Margaret Thatcher's death, Master Ryuho Okawa summoned her spirit to hold a spiritual interview. Her words will prove helpful not only to the United Kingdom, but also to the global economy and governments all over the world.

THE NEW DIPLOMATIC STRATEGIES OF SIR WINSTON CHURCHILL

A SPIRITUAL INTERVIEW WITH THE FORMER PRIME MINISTER REGARDING THE AGE OF PERSEVERANCE

If there is a chance to hear the opinion of Sir Winston Churchill on current international affairs, journalists around the world will probably be interested to hear this. This book made this possible.

ON HAPPINESS REVOLUTION
A SPIRITUAL INTERVIEW WITH HANNAH ARENDT

This spiritual interview dives into the opinions of the German-Jewish political scientist and philosopher, Hannah Ardent. This book touches upon political phenomena, gives advice about political movements, and explains the importance of understanding God's love and justice.

For a complete list of books, visit okawabooks.com

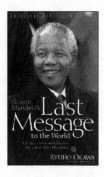

Nelson Mandela's Last Message
A Conversation with Madiba Six Hours After His Death

As Mandela's spirit says in this spiritual interview, God created our souls as thinking energy without color, and that our colorless soul is the basis of our fundamental freedom and equality. In this spiritual interview, Master Ryuho Okawa gives us a glimpse into the mind of this great leader whose undefeated spirit is a message of hope to us all.

Mother Teresa's Current Calling in Heaven
The Saint of the Gutters Delivers Her Experiences of God, Heaven, and Our Mission

In this spiritual interview, Mother Teresa's spirit talks about her astonishing discoveries about God, Heaven, and the mission that people on earth should aim to fulfill through life. She reveals that the other world is a vast place with many levels of angels, that Heaven and Hell exist, and that the reality of the human being is the soul.

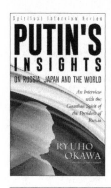

Putin's Insights on Russia, Japan and The World
An Interview with the Guardian Spirit of the President of Russia

In this book, the guardian spirit of President Putin and asks his opinion on the current world leaders, how he looks upon Syrian affairs and the confusion in the EU, and on what he predicts will happen in the next 5 years with the Asian crisis.

For a complete list of books, visit okawabooks.com

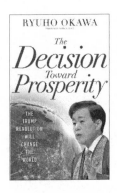

THE DECISION TOWARD PROSPERITY
THE TRUMP REVOLUTION WILL CHANGE THE WORLD

In the book, Okawa talks a lot about Japanese politics as Japan is his mother country, but the universal philosophy behind his words will surely enlighten readers in other countries too. This is the guidebook that will help the world realize prosperity for the next 300 years.

INTO THE STORM OF INTERNATIONAL POLITICS
THE NEW STANDARDS OF THE WORLD ORDER

The world is now seeking a new idea or a new philosophy. In this book, Okawa presents new standards of the world order while giving his own analysis on world affairs concerning the U.S., China, Islamic State and others.

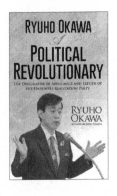

RYUHO OKAWA – A POLITICAL REVOLUTIONARY
THE ORIGINATOR OF ABENOMICS AND FATHER OF THE HAPPINESS REALIZATION PARTY

In this book, Okawa lays down the guiding principles and the ways to breakthrough on the topics of economy, finance, nuclear power plant, foreign diplomacy, social welfare, and society with aging population and a falling birth rate.

For a complete list of books, visit okawabooks.com

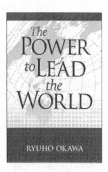

THE POWER TO LEAD THE WORLD

"It is not enough to speak only of ideals; we must envision how this world should be while setting our eyes firmly on things like real politics."

—Master Ryuho Okawa

[This book is available only in local branches and temples. Please refer to the contact information.]

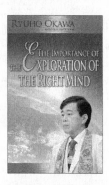

THE IMPORTANCE OF THE EXPLORATION OF THE RIGHT MIND

The basic teaching of Happy Science is 'the exploration of the Right Mind.' The significance of this book is in that it covers the exploration of the Right Mind for the citizen based on a macro-perspective understanding, with whom true sovereignty lies, in addition to the way to explore the Right Mind for the individual religious practitioner.

SPIRITUAL MESSAGES FROM THE GUARDIAN SPIRIT OF RYUHO OKAWA

THE DIVINE VOICE OF SHAKYAMUNI BUDDHA

"The final goal is to realize what you call a 'Buddhaland Utopia.' Of course, this is not an easy task. However, it is important that you keep on making efforts to get close to it, generation after generation."

— Shakyamuni Buddha, Okawa's Guardian spirit

For a complete list of books, visit okawabooks.com

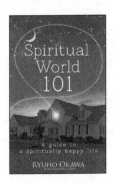

SPIRITUAL WORLD 101
A GUIDE TO A SPIRITUALLY HAPPY LIFE

This book is a spiritual guidebook that will answer all your questions about the spiritual world, with illustrations and diagrams explaining about your guardian spirit and the secrets of God and Buddha. By reading this book, you will be able to understand the true meaning of life and find happiness in everyday life.

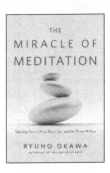

THE MIRACLE OF MEDITATION
OPENING YOUR LIFE TO PEACE, JOY, AND THE POWER WITHIN

This book introduces various types of meditation, including calming meditation, purposeful meditation, reading meditation, reflective meditation, and meditation to communicate with heaven. Through reading and practicing meditation in this book, we can experience the miracle of meditation, which is to start living a life of peace, happiness, and success.

THE MOMENT OF TRUTH
BECOME A LIVING ANGEL TODAY

This book shows that we are essentially spiritual beings and that our true and lasting happiness is not found within the material world but rather in acts of unconditional and selfless love toward the greater world. These pages reveal God's mind, His mercy, and His hope that many of us will become living angels that shine light onto this world.

For a complete list of books, visit okawabooks.com

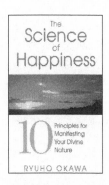

THE SCIENCE OF HAPPINESS
10 PRINCIPLES FOR MANIFESTING YOUR DIVINE NATURE

This book presents the author's 10 essential principles that can serve as a compass for a spiritual life: Happiness, Love, the Mind, Enlightenment, Progress, Wisdom, Utopia, Salvation, Reflection, and Prayer. He shows how following these principles can bring happiness and spiritual growth not only to ourselves but to all those around us.

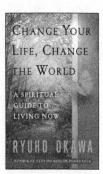

CHANGE YOUR LIFE CHANGE THE WORLD
A SPIRITUAL GUIDE TO LIVING NOW

In this book, the author reveals the true nature of world that we live in; our place in it, and its place in the universe. In possession of this knowledge, each of us is offered the opportunity to bring about a major shift in our own lives and then throughout society by raising our consciousness and that of those around us.

THE UNHAPPINESS SYNDROME
28 HABITS OF UNHAPPY PEOPLE (AND HOW TO CHANGE THEM)

Although we all wish to be happy, many of us fall into a set pattern of failures when we find ourselves in certain circumstances. In this book, Okawa diagnoses the 28 common habits of the Unhappiness Syndrome and offers prescriptions for changing them so that we can cure ourselves of this syndrome.

For a complete list of books, visit okawabooks.com

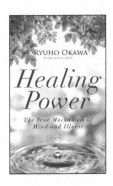

HEALING POWER
THE TRUE MECHANISM OF MIND AND ILLNESS

This book clearly describes the relationship between the mind and illness, and provides you with hints to restore your mental and physical health. Cancer, heart disease, allergy, skin disease, dementia, psychiatric disorder, atopy... Many miracles of healing are happening!

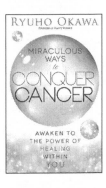

MIRACULOUS WAYS TO CONQUER CANCER
AWAKEN TO THE POWER OF HEALING WITHIN YOU

Why do people get cancer? Why does the number of patients with cancer keep increasing in spite of medical progress? This book reveals how the mind creates cancer and the keys to overcome illnesses. Drive out cancer from your life!

HEALING FROM WITHIN
LIFE-CHANGING KEYS TO CALM, SPIRITUAL, AND HEALTHY LIVING

This book reveals the true causes and remedies for various illnesses that modern medicine doesn't know how to heal. The practical, yet unique cures that this book offers for a variety of medical conditions can help us stay on the path to physical, mental, and spiritual wellbeing.

For a complete list of books, visit okawabooks.com

MESSAGES FROM HEAVEN
WHAT JESUS, BUDDHA, MOSES, AND MUHAMMAD WOULD SAY TODAY

If you could speak to Jesus, Buddha, Moses, or Muhammad, what would you ask? In this book, Okawa shares the spiritual communication he had with these four spirits and the messages they want to share with people living today. The Truths revealed in this book will open your eyes to a level of spiritual awareness, salvation, and happiness that you have never experienced before.

THINK BIG!
BE POSITIVE AND BE BRAVE TO ACHIEVE YOUR DREAMS

Think Big! offers the support and encouragement to shift to new ways of thinking and mastering self-discipline. In addition to his relatable stories and a motivational voice to keep us going, each chapter builds on the next for concrete methodologies that, when added up, are a track to support your dreams, yourself, and your life.

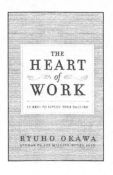

THE HEART OF WORK
10 KEYS TO LIVING YOUR CALLING

In this book, Ryuho Okawa shares 10 key philosophies and goals to live by to guide us through our work lives and triumphantly live our calling. There are key principles that will help you get to the heart of work, manage your time well, prioritize your work, live with long health and vitality, achieve growth, and more.

For a complete list of books, visit okawabooks.com

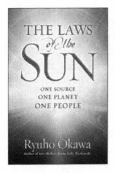

THE LAWS OF THE SUN

ONE SOURCE, ONE PLANET, ONE PEOPLE

IMAGINE IF YOU COULD ASK GOD why He created this world and what spiritual laws He used to shape us—and everything around us. If we could understand His designs and intentions, we could discover what our goals in life should be and whether our actions move us closer to those goals or farther away.

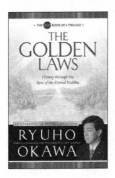

THE GOLDEN LAWS

HISTORY THROUGH THE EYES OF THE ETERNAL BUDDHA

The Golden Laws reveals how Buddha's Plan has been unfolding on earth, and outlines five thousand years of the secret history of humankind. Once we understand the true course of history, we cannot help but become aware of the significance of our spiritual mission in the present age.

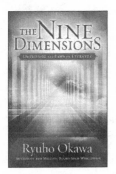

THE NINE DIMENSIONS

UNVEILING THE LAWS OF ETERNITY

This book is a window into the mind of our loving God, who encourages us to grow into greater angels. It reveals His deepest intentions, answering the timely question of why He conceived such a colorful medley of religions, philosophies, sciences, arts, and other forms of expression.

For a complete list of books, visit okawabooks.com

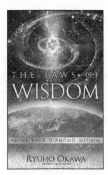

THE LAWS OF WISDOM
SHINE YOUR DIAMOND WITHIN

This book guides you along the path on how to acquire wisdom, so that you can break through any wall you are facing or will confront in your life or in your business. By reading this book, you will be able to avoid getting lost in the flood of information and go beyond the level of just amassing knowledge. You will be able to come up with many great ideas, make effective planning and strategy and develop your leadership skills.

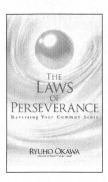

THE LAWS OF PERSEVERANCE
REVERSING YOUR COMMON SENSE

"No matter how much you suffer, the Truth will gradually shine forth as you continue to endure hardships. Therefore, simply strengthen your mind and keep making constant efforts in times of endurance, however ordinary they may be. "

-From Postscript

THE LAWS OF HOPE

THE PATH TO YOUR DREAM, SUCCESS, AND MISSION IN LIFE

This book offers various simple tips to find happiness: how to overcome depressed feelings and live happily; how to improve your relationships; how to choose a good life partner; how to achieve your dreams; and how to achieve success in your private life and in your business. By practicing these tips, you can find hope in your future and you, yourself, will be the light to illuminate the world.

For a complete list of books, visit okawabooks.com

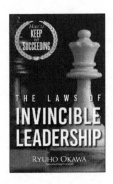

THE LAWS OF INVINCIBLE LEADERSHIP
HOW TO KEEP ON SUCCEEDING

"I wish strongly for all people to attain this true happiness that will persist through the afterlife. With this profound desire, I encourage everyone to aspire to be an invincible winner. I hope that this book will give courage and wisdom to millions of readers today and countless people in the generations to come. "   -From Preface

THE LAWS OF GREAT ENLIGHTENMENT
ALWAYS WALK WITH BUDDHA

In this modern society, we often find ourselves unable to forgive someone and maintain a peaceful mind. However, there are ways to lead a stress-free life and enjoy happiness from within. By understanding the Buddhist concept of "enlightenment," you will gain the power to forgive sins and get to know how to be the master of your own mind.

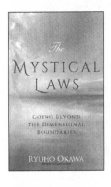

THE MYSTICAL LAWS

GOING BEYOND THE DIMENSIONAL BOUNDARIES

"No matter how much you suffer, the Truth will gradually shine forth as you continue to endure hardships. Therefore, simply strengthen your mind and keep making constant efforts in times of endurance, however ordinary they may be. "
-From Postscript

For a complete list of books, visit okawabooks.com

IRH Movies

Master Okawa is the creator and executive producer of eleven films. These movies have received various awards and recognition around the world.

Movie Titles :

- The Terrifying Revelations of Nostradamus (1994)
- Love Blows Like the Wind (1997)
- The Laws of the Sun (2000)
- The Golden Laws (2003)
- The Laws of Eternity (2006)
- The Rebirth of Buddha (2009)
- The Final Judgement (2012)
- The Mystical Laws (2012)
- The Laws of the Universe – Part 0 (2015)
- I'm Fine, My Angel (2016)
- The World We Live In (2017)

THE MYSTICAL LAWS

The winner of

"2013 Remi Special Jury Award"

for Theatrical Feature Productions in
WorldFest Houston International Film Festival

Other Awards:

– "Palm Beach International Film Festival"
  Nominated for Best Feature Official Selection
– "Asian Film Festival of Dallas" Official selection
– "Proctors 4th Annual Animation Festival"
  Official Selection
– "Buddhist Film Festival Europe" Official Selection
– "Japan-Filmfest Hamburg" Official Selection
– "Monstra,the Lisbon Animated Film Festival"
  Official Selection

Now available on
Video On Demand, **visit**
mystical-laws.com

For more information, visit hspicturesstudio.com

Websites

Ryuho Okawa Official Website

This website introduces Ryuho Okawa to newcomers, shares his profile, amazing achievements, core teachings and how he has inspired many people around the world to happiness.

ryuho-okawa.com

Happy Science Official Website

Official website of Happy Science introducing Master Ryuho Okawa, Happy Science teachings, books, lectures, temples, latest news, etc.

happy-science.org

Okawa Books

Official website of books by Ryuho Okawa. Okawa's spiritual wisdom and philosophies on enlightenment guide you to personal growth and happiness.

okawabooks.com

Spiritual Interview

Official website introducing spiritual interview books by Ryuho Okawa.

okawabooks.com

Notes

Made in the USA
Columbia, SC
27 August 2017